COMFORTABLE IN THE CHAOS

Comfortable in the Chaos

Vincent Bozzino

Libertine Press

© 2022 Vincent Bozzino

Libertine Press
34 Berkley Square
London, UK W1J 5BF

www.libertinepress.com

All rights reserved. No part of this book may be reproduced or used in any manner without written permission, except in the case of brief quotations embodied in social media, critical articles and book reviews.

First published, 2022

Originally written in 2012, with the working title *"The Mask of Orpheus"*.
Second of the *"Youth Poems"* trilogy.

Printed by IngramSpark/LightningSource Inc. in the USA.
Full Editing, Cover Art by Vincent Bozzino

Paperback ISBN 978-1-7392377-5-2
Ebook ISBN 978-1-7392377-6-9

A catalogue record for this title is available from the British Library (London, UK) and the Library of Congress (Washington D.C., USA).

To my soul detractors

You have not succeeded

1

And I started again another time
And I thought it was the last
But the last was always the first
For life never gives you anything
If not fear and pain
And if it gives you something every now and then
Then you have to pay for it

2

Cover your eyes:
I can see your heart.

3

What are you doing over there,
so far away
Come on top of me and take away
The bitterness of the week

- Saturdays

4

I have decided to stay lost in the world
Even if I sink
I let things take me elsewhere
It does not matter where

5

I forgot everything,
everything around me,
the cruel Sunday
the coffee in the morning
the words to say
my sense of defence
when I live with you

I lay my head in this steep valley
a rattling chaos takes my soul
your voice is the map, your eyes are my compass
I want to kiss you
On Monday Mornings
And I hate everyone
on Monday Mornings

I have forgotten everything,
my keys at work
my priorities in the other room
all for you
my *naked muse.*

6

But if suddenly one evening
we looked each other in the eye
we would make good use of it,
a simple and profound use
of us
and the world.

7

Being in tune with life
Feels something accidental
That can happen
Sometimes
To the lucky ones

For the rest
It's just a punishment
Insistence on finishing
- Never in full
- Always in the void

8

I want no pulpit
Nor a power button
Just lend me a bench
Where I can stop and stare
A rose grow
To try and figure why
Being a good person here
Does not love make
But only get you used

9

We are tired of being serious young people,
or *necessarily* happy,
or criminals, jocks or neurotic:
we want to laugh, be innocent,
expect something from tomorrow,
identify, openly ignore.
We don't want to be so sure right away.
We don't want to be so dreamless
right away.

- Millennials

10

A life spent
between the desire to hide and to be noticed
Getting noticed while hiding,
or just as a function of hiding
A slow disappearance
A habit of shade
torbid isolation
The surrender to nothing
Silently waiting
for the silence
to end

- I Am Not Another Spectacle

11

A painful existence
Leaving family as a custom
And spending the rest of adult life
Chasing hopelessly poor versions as a regret

- *Dating*

12

My prison is not made of steel
Nor bricks or bones
My prison is a circle
I engrave in my soul
Anxiety, heavy independence, self-loathing words
My fear of not loving enough in this life
and then dying - worthless -
of this thirst.

13

There is no hope in these towns
No black, no queer and no white, in truth
The only real obstacle is class
Nobody knows how to make it
Unless you're apparent enough

14

Miss the father, miss the sister
Names to my troubles
My walls are chaotic
Loud is silence
I am a daily joker
But the ceiling is always low
I am a daily crawler
In the undersoil
And I crawl back into the hole
I made my permanent home

15

I'm counting on my sad fingers
carnivorous hunger for events
that crosses my spirit
looking for a foothold;
leaves footprints in the dust
too tense to save themselves
and damned, I discover in angst
the hidden etymologies between
the professional walls of society.
And like a carrion, I turned
carefree to be barren of statements.

16

We shall leave on the verge of death
my soul mixed with agony
on this bank that seems a painting
where the river claws the land
and seduces us and carries me
with malignant and benign touch

17

It's the last slap of winter
Freezing brotherly hands
The snow trails and drips on the fearful roofs
Cradled by the frost threatens the fir trees
Falling haughty from the cold sky
The frost on hearts murmurs to the statues

Why do you strike, tear and harass the blessed?

18

When you left
The sky began to cry
You ran away and handed over
gags to the doom makers
to shut me up in the breeze
You're gone
and the wind never blows
and the flock has not yet returned to my farm
In a flash of the stars
you left out in the universe
fluent in a school of fish
or in the dummy flock
You left me
on the brink of bliss
bathed in the sleep of puberty
dying in a longing
without fidelity

19

The rest of a torn page
the trembling of the branches
I travel with a deep hole
that drags black fields over me
and on the tangle, the golden plover
collapsing with its skin
smoothed by a pitiful cry
a book untangles on an avenue

20

Your flower of poetry
your flower of madness
dripping with timid victory
they catch you in the night
to rest between your dead fingers
Lady of the Hundred Lovers
fragile timeless fox
amid the laughter of shared fate
fulfil your stray life
when we were sprinkled
with the incense of your angel wings
full of poetry
Your breath now lives in the poets
timed by the glow of an eternity
where your long trail of love shines by
For you, this and more

21

Comfortable in the chaos
Light the world to ripen and recede
Looking back with anger at today's loss
Rich in the pain, if I shall need

22

Isolation
Half remembered of my home and kites,
Last night, with a lonely sense of fight
Started again to rework my poor life

Rejection
Yielded with blossoms - No free blossoms
Swift to the glare and noise to the town
Boy, may your strength never die

23

Fitness
noth but a fleeting hope
noth but a venomous trip
One last ride
an instant, a month
exasperation

I am but a troubled body

24

Money
Show the world to me
Dreaming by sand with sound
Naked ladies around

Wild and loose in the mass,
Young eyes with a glass
But I resist the empty call
To tumble on, trade all

- Elite Parties

25

Future suffocates me
My demons are health and fame
Be drained by thousands lips
in masochist chains
And held in kin's heart sincerely

26

Living
Bother me
Except eating and getting off
Apathy
Unable to interact successfully
With the ones I like

I don't know where I am going in life
What's missing to make me smile
And I don't understand what's it all about

Sorry, I did not ask this struggle
I was not warned, I can't appreciate the wind
Bring back my self-esteem
Now you know why I always sing

 Writer and musician, Vincent Bozzino (1996) became known as a poet, in Europe, when he was 14 years old, with his first collection *"On My Comet's Tail"*, commended at the Turin International Book Fair and Frankfurt Book Fair. In 2022, *"Love Don't Pay the Bills"* marked his return to publishing verse. A conservatory drop-out, he read Philosophy at University of London and speaks 4 languages.

www.ingramcontent.com/pod-product-compliance
Lightning Source LLC
Chambersburg PA
CBHW070338120526
44590CB00017B/2933